Family Approved Gluten Free Recipes

I'm a Celiac, LLC

www.ImaCeliac.com
Twitter @ImaCeliac

Family Approved Gluten Free Recipes

If it didn't get eaten at our table it isn't in the book!

By Pam Jordan

I'm a Celiac, LLC.

ISBN- 13: 978-1483953199
ISBN -10: 148395319X

Self Published through Creative Space.

Editor: Mary Tomczak
Cover Design: Black Train Designs
Cover Photo: Pam Jordan – Pepperoni Bake

Forward

I met Pam several years ago when she first started blogging. I had been blogging for several years and we met at the Charlotte Gluten-Free Expo in 2011.

Pam is one of those people you immediately love as soon as you meet her. She's genuine, kind, and funny. She has a huge heart for helping people and simply wants to share her gluten-free tips as a busy celiac mom of three.

The recipes in this wonderful gem of a cookbook are real food for real families. They are easy, fast, kid-friendly, familiar, and absolutely delicious. Through her witty and entertaining writing, Pam's cookbook will teach you valuable budget-friendly grocery tips and how to use healthy gluten-free shortcuts to make weeknight meals fast and tasty.

Trust me on this one... with Pam's no-nonsense, joyful approach to cooking gluten-free your family will be begging for more!
Happy Gluten-Free Cooking!

--Carrie S. Forbes

Author of Gingerlemongirl.com and The Everything Gluten-Free Slow Cooker Cookbook, The Everything Gluten-Free College Cookbook, The Everything Gluten-Free Baking Cookbook.

When I was first diagnosed with Celiac Disease, I thought my life was over. All of my eating habits had to change. As I tried to maneuver my way through my new gluten free life, I was frustrated by how complicated some of the recipes were. Ten different flours and fifty different steps...being gluten free couldn't be this hard!

Enter blogs. Blogs became my go-to way to find easy recipes that anyone could follow, including me! And that's what I love about Pam's recipes; they are all easy to prepare. As an avid follower of her blog I'm A Celiac, I am always impressed by how easy Pam's recipes are to follow.

Not to mention that all of her meals are kid tested and approved! If a recipe passes the I'm A Celiac Family Test, then I know my family will love them too! What a blessing to have a collection of recipes that taste delicious and are easy to make!

So get cooking! And enjoy recipes from I'm A Celiac, all in this convenient cookbook. Lucky you!

-- **Marlow Ravelli**

Author of GlutenHatesMe.com

Acknowledgements

First, I want to thank the amazing online Gluten Free community. Without you I would feel so alone. I have made wonderful blog and Twitter friends over the past couple years and I cherish you all!

Second, I need to thank Michael Dickey for being a wonderful business mentor. I have learned so much about leadership, life and business from you. Thank you for helping make all this possible.

Next, I need to thank my wonderful and supportive family! Ever since I have gone Gluten Free everyone has been so encouraging and accommodating. Thanks for eating the weird food I cook and reading my blog.

Lastly, thank you to my fantastic husband, Nick, who eats all the good and bad food I cook. Without your constant support I would not be here. You make me a better person! And to our children, I am so blessed and honored to be your mommy!

Table of Contents

Introduction   10
My Story   11
Product Highlights   13

Breakfast   15
Appetizers   25
Main Dishes   33
Slow Cooker & Freezer Meals   51
Side Dishes   63
Desserts   69

Index   81

Introduction

I'm a Celiac. I'm also a wife and a working mom to three young kids living Gluten Free. Dinnertime comes once a day and we are all faced with the same old question, *"What's for dinner?"* As a person with Celiac Disease or Gluten Sensitivity the answer to that question isn't always easy. Driving through a fast food restaurant or ordering a pizza is NOT always a safe option.

After a few years living Gluten Free I have compiled a good list of recipes that are family approved and easy to make. These recipes take advantage of pre-packaged products combined with simple ingredients. These recipes do not have too many ingredients. They take help from pre-packaged products and don't use strange ingredients like artichoke flowers or ginger root (while both of those are fine ingredients they are just not found in my pantry or fridge).

These recipes are also very easy to customize to your family's likes and other food sensitivities. Since the only obstacle in our house is Gluten our meals do have soy, egg, dairy, nuts and other allergens. Please feel free to make any necessary adjustments to make these meals safe for your family.

Enjoy!

My Story

The road to my Celiac Disease diagnosis took 15 years of "tummy problems" and multiple doctor visits.

It all started for me in high school. Some time during my sophomore year I started having issues with my stomach (read diarrhea). Many of my meals just went right through me. After some tests a doctor told me I had Irritable Bowel Syndrome or IBS. So he gave me some meds and sent me on my way. It got to the point where going out to eat at a restaurant was just a waste of money, as I would only "rent" my meal. As it would make a quick exit as soon as I got home.

I got a handle on things and could isolate certain foods that would set me off more than others. I still had issues but it wasn't as bad. Then the depression showed up a year later. There is a history of depression in my family so I'm not blaming it all on the Celiac Disease but I'm sure it enhanced my likelihood of getting it. I remember having so many foggy days of limited emotion. After another doctor visit I was given "happy pills" at age sixteen. I stayed on them for more than twelve years.

When my husband and I decided to start our family I went to the doctor to get checked out to make sure everything was ok, since I had a history of crazy cycles. After more tests I found out I had Polycystic Ovary Syndrome or PCOS. It causes problems with fertility so that meant more meds. Luckily after two months we were pregnant with our first child, a girl.

So at this point I had IBS, depression, and infertility issues and had meds for all of them!

In November of 2010 during a visit with my gastroenterologist I told him to test me for everything he could think of. I was tired of frequenting the bathroom and wanted some real answers. I refused to take IBS as an answer for why food had been my enemy for so long. A blood test for Celiac Disease came back with a rating of "moderate to strong". To get a complete diagnosis I had to have an upper endoscopy so they could biopsy my small intestines. This biopsy was done right before Christmas. January 4, 2011 my life changed with a call and email from the doctor saying I was confirmed to have Celiac Disease.

Finally I had the answer to all my health issues. Celiac Disease causes diarrhea, depression and infertility. The cure or management of the disease is a Gluten Free diet. A simple solution but a difficult and major life change. I quickly learned all I could about Gluten, where it hides, how to avoid it and what I actually could eat. My husband and I joke about his first reaction to learning what Gluten was. He said, "There is no way we can do this". Now he is my biggest advocate and food label reader.

Within two weeks of going Gluten Free I felt like a NEW PERSON! I had more energy, zero tummy problems and just felt better overall. I'm eating better than I ever have, I'm exercising and I feel great! Since going Gluten Free we even got pregnant with twins and I had a healthy pregnancy.

Being Diagnosed with Celiac Disease answered so many questions for me. Living Gluten Free has freed me to live life and enjoy food again! Eating Gluten Free has been a blessing to my family and me. Thank you for taking the time to share in our journey.

Product Highlights

I take a lot of help from packaged Gluten Free products. In a perfect world I would make everything from scratch but there aren't enough hours in the day. There are also a growing number of wonderful Gluten Free products on the market that I take full advantage of and support.

ALWAYS read labels because manufactures do make changes to their ingredients!

Here are some of my favorites and pantry staples.

Bread
Rudi's
Three Bakers
Udi's

Gluten Free Flour Mixes
Jules Gluten Free
Bloomfield Farms
Pamela's
Gluten Free Bisquick

Pie Crust (frozen)
Whole Foods brand

Pasta
Tinkyada

Sauces
Soy Sauce – San-J Tamari
Cream of Chicken/Mushroom Soup – Pacific Natural Foods
Ranch Dressing – Hidden Valley
BBQ Sauce – Bone Suckin Sauce
Worcestershire Sauce – Lea & Perrins

Cereal
General Mills Chex
Post Fruity Peebles
Envirokids Organic Gorilla Munch
Bob's Red Mill Quick Cooking Oats

Bread Crumbs
Tall Papa

Granola
Trader Joe's brand
Bakery on Main

Crackers
Crunchmaster
Glutino

Macaroni and Cheese - Boxed
Annie's
Trader Joe's brand

Where We Shop
Aldi – Great Gluten Free labeling
Trader Joe's – Great Gluten Free labeling
Whole Foods - Great Gluten Free labeling
Local Grocery Stores
Farmer's Market

Breakfast Recipes

Banana Pancakes   16
Egg Frittatas   17
Pumpkin Chocolate Chip Muffins   18
Sausage Breakfast Skillet   19
Sausage Balls   20
Overnight Oatmeal Smoothies   21
Greek Yogurt Pancakes   22
Bacon Ranch Puffs   23

Banana Pancakes

What You Need

1 cup GF Bisquick
1 cup milk
2 tbsp vegetable oil
1 egg
1/8 tsp GF vanilla extract
2 ripe bananas
a dash of cinnamon
Optional - chocolate chips, raisins or pecans

How to Make It

1. Cut up bananas and put in Ziploc bag and sqeeeezzze! (kids like this part)
2. Mix the remaining ingredients in a bowl. Cut a corner off of the plastic bag with the bananas and add to batter. The batter will be lumpy.
3. Put 1/4 cup of batter on a warmed, lightly greased griddle. Add chocolate chips or nuts if you want.
4. Flip when bubbles come through batter. Cook pancakes about 1-2 minutes on each side.

Makes 14 pancakes

Egg Frittata

What You Need

6 large eggs
½ cup milk
1 cup shredded cheddar cheese
¾ cup of chopped vegetables (*zucchini, squash, tomatoes, onion and green pepper are some favorites*)
Pinch of salt and pepper
¼ cup chopped meat (ham, turkey or bacon)
1 Gluten Free piecrust - I use Whole Foods brand.

How to Make It

1. Preheat oven to 350 degrees.
2. Mix the eggs, milk, salt and pepper together.
3. Add the veggies, meat, and cheese. Stir well.
4. Pour into piecrust.
5. Bake for 35-40 minutes until firm.
6. Let cool and set up for 10 minutes then serve.

Tips: This heats up very well for great breakfast leftovers.

Pumpkin Chocolate Chip Muffins

What You Need

1 cup light brown sugar
¼ cup vegetable oil or applesauce
2 eggs
1 cup canned pumpkin
¼ cup water (May not need all)
1 ½ cups Gluten Free Baking Mix (Like Pamela's)
¾ tsp baking powder
½ tsp baking soda
1 tsp ground cinnamon
¼ tsp salt
½ tsp ground nutmeg
1 cup semisweet chocolate chips

How to Make It

1. Preheat the oven to 375 degrees F. Lightly spray paper cups with cooking spray.
2. Mix sugar, oil, eggs, pumpkin and water together. In separate bowl mix together the baking mix, baking soda, baking powder, spices and salt.
3. Add wet mixture and stir in chocolate chips.
4. Fill liners 2/3 full with batter.
5. Bake in preheated oven for 20 minutes.

Makes 18 muffins

Sausage Breakfast Skillet

What You Need

4 cubed potatoes
2 tbsp butter or oil
½ green pepper chopped
½ onion chopped
1 lb GF sausage - Like Jimmy Dean
¼ cup milk
7 eggs
Seasoned salt

Topping:
Mild cheddar cheese shredded

How to Make It

1. Melt butter in a skillet over medium heat. Once heated add potatoes and season salt.
2. Cook covered for 10 minutes, stirring occasionally. Once cooked remove the potatoes from the skillet.
3. Add sausage, onions and peppers to the skillet. Cook until sausage is no longer pink.
4. In another bowl mix together the milk and eggs.
5. Move the sausage and veggies to the side of the skillet. Pour in eggs to the empty space and scramble.
6. When the eggs are cooked add the potatoes back to the skillet and heat for 5 minutes.
7. Serve with shredded cheese!

Sausage Balls

What You Need

2 cups GF Bisquick
1 lb GF sausage
3 cups sharp cheddar cheese shredded
a splash of milk

How to Make It

1. Using your fingers mix together the Bisquick and the sausage.
2. Then mix in the cheese.
3. Add the milk if the mixture is not sticking together. You don't want wet dough just moist enough to stick together.
4. Form into balls and bake on parchment lined baking sheet for 25 minutes at 350 degrees.

Makes 2 dozen

Overnight Oatmeal Smoothie

What You Need

¼ cup GF oats
1 ½ tsp chia seeds
1 cup milk
1/3 cup yogurt (regular or Greek)
1 cup fruit of choice (frozen or fresh)

How to Make It

1. In a smoothie blender mix the oats and chia seeds. Grind it up until it is fine.
2. Add the rest of the ingredients and blend.
3. Refrigerate overnight or for at least 4 hours.

Tips: You could also freeze them in mason jars and thaw when ready to drink. You can add some juice for additional flavor.

Greek Yogurt Pancakes

What You Need

1 6oz container of GF Greek yogurt – plain or flavored
2 eggs
1 ½ cups of GF Bisquick
¾ cup of milk
a splash of GF vanilla

How to Make It

1. Heat up your griddle and lightly grease.
2. In a bowl whisk together the yogurt and the eggs.
3. Then mix in the Bisquick, milk and vanilla.
4. Pour 1/3 cup of batter on the griddle.
5. They take about 3 minutes per side.

Makes 13 pancakes

Bacon Ranch Puffs

What You Need

3 pieces of cooked bacon chopped
¾ cup of GF Bisquick
1 cup shredded sharp cheddar cheese
2 tbsp GF Ranch dressing
¼ cup of milk

How to Make It

1. Heat oven to 400 degrees.
2. Mix together all the ingredients except the milk.
3. Slowly add in milk until you get a mixture that will stay together, but you still want it kind of dry. You aren't looking for pancake batter consistency.
4. Scoop into small balls and bake on parchment paper for 12-14 minutes.

Makes 12 puffs.

Appetizers

Onion Rings   26
Bacon Cheeseburger Puffs   27
Baked Mozzarella Sticks   28
Baked Potato Skins   29
Broccoli and Quinoa Bites   30
Corn Dog Muffins   31
Quinoa Pizza Treats   32

Onion Rings

What You Need
1 egg
¼ cup vegetable oil
1 ½ cups milk
2 cup GF Flour
½ tsp salt
1 tsp baking powder
1 Vidalia onion cut into rings
1 ½ tbsp seasoned salt

oil for frying - I use vegetable

How to Make It

1. Heat oil in fryer to 350 degrees.
2. Put cut onion rings into an ice bath.
3. Mix egg, oil and milk together. Add 1 cup flour, baking powder, salt and ½ tsp seasoned salt. You may need to add more milk if the batter is too thick.
4. In a separate bowl mix together 1 cup GF flour and 1 tsp seasoned salt.
5. Take onion ring out of water bath and put in dry flour mix.
6. Put onion ring in batter to coat
7. Put in fryer. Turn them halfway through to get both sides cooked. Takes about 3 minutes.
8. Put cooked onion rings onto plate with paper towel

Serve with your favorite sauce

Bacon Cheeseburger Puffs

What You Need

½ lb ground beef
1 tbsp chopped onion

3 pieces of cooked bacon chopped up
1 ½ cups of GF Bisquick
2 cups shredded sharp cheddar cheese
1/3 cup of milk - may need a splash or two more

How to Make It:

1. Heat oven to 400 degrees.
2. Brown beef and cook onions. Drain fat.
3. Mix together all the ingredients except the milk.
4. Slowly add in milk until you get a mixture that will stay together but you still want it kind of dry. You aren't looking for pancake batter consistency.
5. Scoop into small balls and bake on parchment paper for 12-14 minutes.

Makes 20 puffs

Baked Mozzarella Sticks

What You Need

12 part-skim mozzarella sticks
1 egg
2 tbsp GF flour
6 tbsp GF bread crumbs
2 tbsp grated parmesan cheese

How to Make It

1. Cut mozzarella sticks in half and freeze for at least an hour on parchment paper on a cookie sheet.
2. Get your prepping bowls ready.
   1 with the GF flour
   1 with a beaten egg
   1 with the GF bread crumbs and parmesan cheese
3. Pull out frozen cheese sticks and take them through the prep bowls. Flour - egg - bread crumbs.
4. Place back on the parchment paper and freeze for at least 10 minutes.
5. Heat oven to 400 degrees.
6. Grease a foil covered cookie sheet.
7. Transfer the frozen sticks to the foil sheet and cook for 3 minutes on one side then flip and bake for another 3 minutes. Keep an eye on them!

Serve with GF marinara sauce

Tips: If you don't want to cook them all at one time just freeze them already breaded for later.

Baked Potato Skins

What You Need

5-7 Baking potatoes
3 tbsp of vegetable oil
Salt and pepper
Dash of paprika
Dash of garlic salt
1 tbsp grated parmesan cheese

Toppings:
Cheese
GF Bacon
GF Ranch

How to Make It:

1. Bake potatoes for an hour at 350 degrees.
2. Let sit for 10 minutes while you heat the oven to 450 degrees.
3. Slice the potatoes in half and scoop out the insides. Make sure you leave enough on the inside to create your bowl shape. (You can save the insides for mashed potatoes)
4. Mix oil and seasoning together and brush onto potato skins.
5. Bake at 450 for 7 minutes.
6. Take out and fill with toppings.
7. Cook for another 2-5 minutes or until cheese is bubbly. Top with sour cream and you are good to go!

Tips: Making extra empty skins are also a good idea. They can be heated and filled later for a snack.

Broccoli and Quinoa Bites

What You Need

12 oz bag of frozen broccoli
½ cup uncooked Quinoa
½ cup grated carrots
1 ½ cups cheddar cheese shredded
3 eggs
¼ cup GF ranch dressing
1 slice of toasted GF bread cut up
Salt and pepper

How to Make It

1. Cook the Quinoa according to the instructions on the box.
2. Heat the oven to 375 degrees.
3. Chop up the broccoli and mix with carrots.
4. Add cheese, egg and dressing to veggie mixture.
5. When Quinoa is done add with toast to mixture.
6. Cook in greased muffin tins for 10-15 minutes.

Makes 18 muffins

Corn Dog Muffins

What You Need

GF Corn muffin mix – make enough for 6 regular size
muffins
3 hot dogs

How to Make It

1. Heat oven to 400 degrees.
2. Spray mini-muffin pan with cooking oil.
3. Mix corn muffin mix as directed.
4. Cut hot dogs into small 1 inch pieces, about 6
   pieces per hot dog.
5. Fill muffin tins half full with corn mix and place
   hot dog in the center.
6. Bake at 400 for 9 minutes.

Serve with the dip of your choice.

Quinoa Pizza Treats

What You Need

1 cup cooked Quinoa
½ cup chopped turkey pepperoni
½ cup shredded mozzarella cheese
1 tbsp grated parmesan cheese
1 tsp Italian seasoning
2 eggs

How to Make It

1. Heat oven to 350 degrees
2. Spray mini muffin tin with cooking spray
3. Mix all ingredients together.
4. Fill muffin tin.
5. Cook for 15 - 20 minutes.

Serve with red pasta sauce or ranch!

Main Dishes

Baked Ziti   34
Beef non-Stew   35
Chicken Spaghetti   36
Chicken Fried Rice   37
Lasagna   38
Meatloaf   39
Mexican Shepherd Pie   40
One Dish Wonder   41
Parmesan Pork Chops   42
Pasta Bake   43
Pepperoni Bake   44
Scalloped Potato and Hamburger   45
Shepherd's Pie   46
Stuffed Pepper Casserole   47
Stuffed Peppers   48
Chicken Tater Tot Casserole   49
Enchilada Casserole   50

I have salt and pepper listed in most of my recipes but list no amounts. Please use as much or as little as your family prefers.

<u>One Dish Meals</u>
Whenever possible I try to cook one dish meals. To me this means meat, vegetables and a starch all cooked together. This saves time and you don't have to worry about timing everything so it is all finished at the same time.

Baked Ziti

What You Need

2 jars of 16oz GF pasta sauce
1 lb ground beef
½ onion, chopped
1 clove garlic minced or chopped
18 oz bag of GF pasta
15 oz Ricotta
1 egg
¼ cup grated parmesan cheese
3 cups shredded mozzarella cheese
oregano to taste

How to Make It

1. Heat oven to 375 degrees.
2. Brown beef with onions and garlic, drain fat. Add sauce to meat.
3. While pasta is cooking (only cook for ¾ time on package), mix ricotta, egg, oregano, parmesan and 1.5 cups of mozzarella cheese in a bowl.
4. Drain pasta and mix into cheese mixture.
5. Cover bottom of 9x12 casserole dish with some of the sauce.
6. Then add a layer of the pasta/ cheese mixture, then add a sauce layer, repeat. Cover the dish with the remaining mozzarella cheese.
7. Cover with foil and bake for 30 minutes. Bake uncovered for another 10 minutes.

Beef Non-Stew

What You Need

1 lb ground beef
1 can green beans
1 pound potatoes, cubed
½ cup chopped carrots
2 GF beef bouillon cubes
1 ½ to 2 cups water

How to Make It

1. Brown beef in skillet, drain fat.
2. Add potatoes, veggies, bouillon and water. You want to add just enough water to cover the meat and veggies.
3. Cover and cook on low to medium heat for 30 minutes. When the potatoes are cooked you are ready to go!

Serve with GF corn muffins, cheese and sour cream. Onion or green peppers and even corn would be great in this as well.

Chicken Spaghetti

What You Need

3 Chicken breasts
1 box GF Cream of Mushroom soup
8 oz Velveeta cheese
1 can of Rotel diced tomatoes and green chilies
1 cup of shredded cheddar cheese
Salt and pepper

Gluten Free Pasta 16oz bag

How to Make It

1. Boil the chicken until cooked, about 20 minutes. Remove from water and chop.
2. Boil the water and cook your GF pasta.
3. In a skillet mix together the chicken, soup, cheeses and Rotel.
4. Cook the pasta and drain.
5. Mix the pasta with the cheese sauce and serve.

Tip: This dish can also be baked at 350 degrees for 30 minutes. Just cook your pasta for 3/4 of the time listed on the bag.

Chicken Fried Rice

What You Need

2 large chicken breasts, cubed or sliced into small pieces
1/3 cup Gluten Free Soy sauce
1/2 bag of frozen stir fry veggies
1/4 onion, chopped
2 cups cooked brown rice
1 egg
1/3 cup cooking oil
1 tbsp butter
Pepper to taste

How to Make It

1. Heat oil and butter in skillet on medium high heat.
2. Add frozen veggies to skillet with onions, cover and cook for 5 minutes.
3. Put chicken in skillet and cook for 4 minutes.
4. Move contents to one side of the skillet; put the egg in and scramble.
5. Add rice and soy sauce to mixture.
6. Cook for 5 minutes and serve!

Tip: For more flavor, marinate the chicken in your favorite GF soy sauce or teriyaki sauce for a few hours before cooking.

Lasagna

What You Need

1 lb ground beef
1 box Gluten Free lasagna noodles - I use De Boles
2 eggs
32 oz red GF pasta sauce
1 ½ cups ricotta
1 ½ cups cottage cheese
½ cup grated parmesan cheese
2 cups shredded mozzarella cheese
Salt and pepper

How to Make It

1. Heat oven to 375 degrees.
2. Brown beef, drain fat and heat with red pasta sauce.
3. Mix eggs, ricotta/cottage cheese, parmesan and salt and pepper in a bowl.
4. In a 9x12 or 2 9x9 pans layer uncooked lasagna noodles, cheese mixture, meat/ sauce mixture, mozzarella cheese and repeat. Cover with remaining mozzarella cheese.
5. Cover with foil and bake for 40 minutes. Let set for 10 minutes then serve.

Tips: If you make 2 9x9 pans it is easy to freeze one for later. Just line the pan with foil with enough on the sides to cover the top. Then layer the ingredients as listed above. Only cook the one to be frozen for 25 minutes. Once it cools down put it in the freezer. Once frozen remove the casserole dish and the foil will hold the frozen meal. When time to eat cook for 30 minutes at 375.

Meatloaf

What You Need

1 lb ground beef
1/2 cup milk
2 eggs
2 slices of toasted GF bread ends, chopped up
1/2 onion, chopped
Salt & pepper

1/4 cup brown sugar
1/2 cup ketchup

How to Make It

1. Heat oven to 350 degrees. Spray loaf pan or muffin tins with cooking spray.
2. Mix all ingredients together minus the ketchup and brown sugar. Mix the ketchup and brown sugar in a separate bowl.
3. Fill the loaf pan or muffin tins with the meatloaf mixture and top with ketchup and brown sugar.
4. Bake for 35 minutes in muffin tins or 50 minutes in loaf pan.

Mexican Shepherd Pie

What You Need

1 lb ground beef
1 packet of Gluten Free taco seasoning
3/4 cup water
2 cups prepared Gluten Free cornbread mixture
1 can diced tomatoes, drained
1/2 onion chopped
1 can corn drained
3/4 cup shredded cheddar cheese

How to Make It

1. Heat oven to 400 degrees.
2. Brown beef with onion in a skillet, drain fat.
3. Add corn, tomatoes, water and taco seasoning to meat and cook on medium for 5 minutes.
4. While this is cooking prepare your cornbread. Mine called for 1/2 cup water, 1 egg and 1 cup cornbread mix.
5. Put meat and veggie mix in a casserole dish, cover with cheese and cornbread mixture.
6. Cook for 20 to 25 minutes or until cornbread is cooked.

Top with more cheese, salsa, or sour cream!

One Dish Wonder

What You Need

3 to 4 chicken breasts
2 cups frozen green beans
¾ cup carrots
3 red potatoes, cubed
½ stick of butter - melted
½ packet of GF Italian seasoning
1 tbsp chopped onion
Salt & pepper
Seasoned salt
Garlic powder

How to Make It

1. Heat oven to 350 degrees.
2. Spray 9x13 dish with cooking spray.
3. Place the green beans and carrots on one side of the dish, chicken in the middle and potatoes on the other side.
4. Top chicken with Italian seasoning. Top green beans / carrots with salt and pepper, garlic powder and half the onion. Top potatoes with salt and pepper, season salt and remaining onion.
5. Pour melted butter over all items.
6. Cover with foil and bake for 1 hour.

Tips: You can easily switch out any vegetables that you have on hand for this dish! If you are using frozen chicken you may need to add another 10 minutes of cooking time. This is a wonderful and easy dish to take to a neighbor or new mom.

Parmesan Pork Chops

What You Need

4 boneless pork chops
½ cup GF bread crumbs
¾ cup parmesan cheese (Combine shredded and grated)
1 tbsp olive oil
1 egg
¼ cup GF flour
Salt & pepper
Seasoned salt
Garlic powder

How to Make It

1. Heat oven to 400 degrees.
2. Put flour, salt and pepper in a shallow bowl. Put parmesan, GF bread crumbs, season salt and garlic powder in a second bowl. Put the egg in a third bowl.
3. Pat the chops dry with a paper towel. Coat chops in flour, egg, then parmesan mixture. Let rest while you heat the olive oil in a skillet over medium high heat.
4. Brown the pork chops for 2 minutes on each side.
5. Then bake on a greased cookie sheet for 15 minutes.

Tips: This could easily be topped with GF red pasta sauce, mozzarella cheese and served over GF spaghetti noodles.

Pasta Bake

What You Need

1 lb GF pasta
1 jar GF red pasta sauce
½ jar GF white pasta sauce
1 lb ground beef
¼ chopped onion
1 cup shredded cheddar cheese
¼ cup grated parmesan cheese
4 oz cream cheese

How to Make It

1. Heat oven to 350 degrees.
2. Brown beef with onions and drain fat.
3. Mix pasta sauces with beef and onions - let simmer 10 minutes while you cook the pasta.
4. Rinse the pasta with cold water and mix the cream cheese and parmesan cheese into the pasta.
5. Layer the pasta in a 9x12 casserole dish, cover with meat/sauce mixture and top with shredded cheese.
6. Cook for 25 minutes until cheese is bubbling.

Pepperoni Bake

What You Need

12 oz GF pasta
1 16 oz jar red GF pasta sauce
1 ½ cups of shredded mozzarella cheese
3 oz chopped GF pepperonis (Hormel is a good GF brand)
½ cup of GF bread crumbs

How to Make It

1. Heat oven to 350 degrees.
2. Cook pasta al dente, about ¾ the time listed on the bag.
3. Once pasta is done mix with sauce, cheese and pepperonis in a casserole dish.
4. Top with bread crumbs and cook for 25 minutes.

Scalloped Potato and Hamburger

What You Need

1 lb ground beef or turkey
6 medium potatoes, sliced
½ medium onion, chopped
Garlic salt and pepper
1 tbsp GF Worcestershire sauce
1 cup milk
¾ cup shredded cheddar cheese
1 12oz box GF cream of mushroom soup

How to Make It

1. Preheat oven to 350 degrees.
2. In a skillet brown meat with onions, drain fat
3. Season meat with garlic salt and pepper to taste. Add Worcestershire sauce.
4. In a separate bowl combine soup and milk.
5. Add soup mix and potatoes to the meat and pour into casserole dish. Cover with cheese.
6. Cook covered for 45 minutes or until potatoes are tender.

Shepherd's Pie

What You Need

1 lb ground beef
¼ chopped onion
1 can drained corn
1 can drained green beans
1 egg
1 tbsp brown sugar
1 tbsp GF Worcestershire
2 tbsp ketchup
2 cups cooked mashed potatoes
1 cup shredded cheddar cheese

How To Make It

1. Heat oven to 350 degrees.
2. Brown beef with onions, drain fat.
3. Prepare potatoes per the package.
4. In a small bowl mix together egg, Worcestershire sauce, brown sugar and ketchup.
5. When beef is cooked through add the can of drained corn and green beans.
6. Once the potatoes are ready stir wet ingredients into beef mixture. You don't want them to sit in the skillet very long because you don't want the eggs to start to scramble.
7. Pour meat/ veggie mixture into casserole dish, top with potatoes, and cover with cheese.
8. Bake for 25 minutes.

Stuffed Pepper Casserole

What You Need

1 lb ground beef
½ white onion, chopped
1 large green pepper, chopped
1 jar (24 oz) GF red pasta sauce
2 cups cooked brown rice
¾ cup shredded cheddar cheese
Salt and pepper

How to Make It

1. Heat oven to 350 degrees.
2. Brown beef with chopped onion and chopped pepper, drain fat.
3. Add rice, half of the cheese and sauce to the skillet. Stir and cook until cheese starts to melt.
4. Put mixture into a casserole dish and cover with remaining cheese.
5. Cook for 30 minutes.

Stuffed Peppers

What You Need

1 lb ground beef
4 bell peppers
½ onion chopped
2 cloves garlic, diced
1 can diced tomatoes, drained
2 cups cooked brown rice or 1 cup Quinoa
2/3 cup shredded cheddar cheese
Salt / pepper
Garlic salt
Oregano

How to Make It

1. Preheat oven to 350 degrees.
2. Brown beef with onions and garlic, drain fat.
3. Add tomatoes and the seasoning. Let cook 5 minutes.
4. Cut tops off peppers and clean out seeds.
5. Add rice to beef mixture and spoon into peppers. Top with cheese.
6. Cook for 30 minutes.

Chicken Tater Tot Casserole

What You Need

½ bag of 32 oz frozen GF tater tots
2 cups of cubed chicken
8 ozs of frozen green beans
½ cup of GF ranch dressing
1 12oz box of GF cream of chicken
1/3 cup of milk
1 cup shredded cheddar cheese
Salt & pepper

How to Make It

1. Heat oven to 375 degrees.
2. Lightly grease your casserole dish.
3. Mix together the chicken, green beans, ranch, cream of chicken, milk, seasoning and cheese.
4. Pour into casserole dish and top with tater tots.
5. Cook for 35 minutes.

Enchilada Casserole

What You Need

2 cups chopped cooked chicken
½ packet of GF enchilada seasoning
½ cup of water
8 oz tomato sauce
1 can of diced tomatoes
½ can of black beans, drained

1½ cups shredded cheddar cheese
¾ cup sour cream
GF corn tortillas

How to Make It

1. Heat oven to 350 degrees.
2. In a pot mix together chicken, seasoning, water, sauce, tomatoes and beans.
3. Heat over medium for 10 minutes.
4. In a small pot melt the cheese and sour cream. Stir and melt over medium heat.
5. In a casserole dish layer corn tortillas, chicken mixture, cheese mixture and repeat.
6. Bake for 25 minutes.

Tip: You could also use 1 lb of seasoned ground beef with this recipe instead of chicken.

Slow Cooker & Freezer Meals

Chicken with White Sauce   53
Crock Pot Lasagna   54
Teriyaki Chicken   55
Sausage and Peppers   56
BBQ Chicken   57
BBQ Pork Chops   58
Chicken Chili   59
Hawaiian Pork   60
Beef Roast   61

Freezer Meal Tips

1. Shop the weekly sales. Many times you can get meat BOGO and vegetables go on sale often.
2. Chop all the veggies first then organize the meat. I have all my chopped veggies in bowls so I can grab handfuls to fill my bags.
3. Mark your bags before you fill them.
4. You could easily add more meat to each bag if you are feeding more people.
5. It is easy and a big time saver to make multiple freezer meals at one time. Many of the ingredients cross over so you save time when you compile many meals at one time.
6. The day before you want to use a meal put it in the fridge to defrost. At lunchtime put it in the crock pot.

How to Make Freezer Meals

Step one - chop up veggies
Step two - label bags with cooking instructions
Step three - assemble meals in bags
Step four - freeze the meals

Chicken with White Sauce

What You Need

2-3 chicken breasts
2 tbsp butter
1 packet GF Italian salad dressing mix

1 box GF cream of chicken
8oz cream cheese

How To Make It

1. Cut up chicken and put in slow cooker with butter and dry Italian mix. Cook on low for 4 hours or high for 2 hours. YES - that is all; do not put in the other ingredients yet.
2. About 45 minutes before time to eat mix in the cream of chicken and cream cheese.
3. Turn up to high and let it mix together. Stir and you are done!

   You can serve it over GF pasta or rice.

Crock Pot Lasagna

What You Need

1 lb ground beef
2 cans (12oz) tomato sauce
2 cans (7oz) tomato paste
1 tbsp Italian seasoning mix
1 diced tomato
1/4 chopped green pepper
1 - 2 sliced medium sized zucchini
1 box GF rice lasagna noodles (uncooked)
1 cup cottage cheese
1 cup ricotta cheese
1 egg
1/3 cup grated parmesan cheese
1 cup mozzarella cheese

How to Make It

1. Brown beef and drain fat. Add tomato sauce, paste, seasoning, and veggies to the skillet.
2. Put on low and simmer for at least 10 minutes while you get everything else together.
3. Whisk the cheeses and egg together in a bowl.
4. Layers for the crock pot: tomato sauce, double layer of noodles (uncooked), cheese mixture, and repeat.
5. Cook on low for 4 hours.
6. For the last hour top with more mozzarella cheese.

Teriyaki Chicken

Freezer Meal

What You Need

2 cups carrots chopped
1 onion chopped
1 can pineapple with juice
3 or 4 chicken breasts
½ cup GF teriyaki sauce

How to Make It

1. Mix all the ingredients together and put in crock pot.
2. Cook for 4 hours on low.
3. Serve with rice.

Sausage and Peppers

Freezer Meal

What You Need

4 GF chicken sausages sliced
1 green pepper chopped
2 multi-colored peppers chopped
1 onion chopped
1 can diced tomatoes
Splash of EVOO
1 tbsp Italian seasoning
1/4 tsp Garlic salt

How to Make It

1. Mix all the ingredients together and put in crock pot.
2. Cook for 5 hours on low.
3. Serve with GF pasta.

Skillet Option
This meal can also be cooked in a skillet. Just cover and cook for 30 minutes over medium heat.

BBQ Chicken

Freezer Meal

What You Need

3 to 4 chicken breasts
1 green pepper chopped
1 multi-colored pepper chopped
1 onion chopped
3 chopped red potatoes (big pieces)
1 can tomato sauce
1 tbsp brown sugar
1 tbsp GF Worcestershire sauce
1 tbsp mustard
1/4 tsp garlic salt

How to Make It

1. Mix all the ingredients together and put in crock pot.
2. Cook for 4 hours on low.
3. Serve with rice.

BBQ Pork Chops

Freezer Meal

What You Need

3 to 4 boneless pork chops
1 green pepper chopped
1 cup chopped carrots
2 cups chopped celery
½ cup GF BBQ sauce

How to Make It

1. Mix all the ingredients together and put in crock pot.
2. Cook for 4 hours on low.
3. Serve with rice or pasta.

Mexican Chicken Chili

What You Need

2 large frozen chicken breasts
1 can corn, drained
1 can black beans, drained
1 16oz GF salsa
4oz cream cheese

How to Make It

1. Put the first four ingredients in the slow cooker at lunchtime on low (yes the frozen chicken too!) or for 4 hours on low.
2. 30 minutes before you are ready to eat pull the chicken out and use forks to pull it apart.
3. Put it back in the slow cooker with the cream cheese.
4. Let cook on high for 20 minutes.

   Serve with rice, tortilla chips, corn tortillas or just eat it straight!

Hawaiian Pork

Freezer Meal

What You Need

1/2 cup ketchup
1 tsp paprika
1/2 cup orange juice
2 tbsp honey
1 garlic clove
1 tbsp GF soy sauce
1 cup zucchini chopped
1 cup chopped carrots
1 chopped onion
1 cup chopped peppers
4 pork chops

How to Make It

1. Mix all the ingredients together and put in crock pot.
2. Cook 4 hours on low.
3. Serve with rice.

Beef Roast

What You Need

3 to 4 lb beef sirloin roast
1 box of GF cream of mushroom soup
1 tbsp GF Worcestershire
1 cup water
4 cubed potatoes
1 cup chopped carrots
1 chopped onion

Oil
Salt and pepper

How to Make it

1. Heat oil in skillet over medium high heat.
2. Season both sides of the roast with salt and pepper.
3. Place in hot skillet. Brown on each side for 5 minutes.
4. Place vegetables in bottom of slow cooker.
5. Mix together soup, water and Worcestershire in a bowl.
6. Place browned roast over vegetables and cover with liquids.
7. Cook on low for 8 hours.

Side Dishes

Summer Veggie Medley   64
Veggie Mac n Cheese   65
Green Bean Casserole   66
Sweet Potato Casserole   67
Ranch Potatoes   68

Summer Veggie Medley

What You Need

2 yellow squash - sliced
2 zucchini - sliced
2 roma tomatoes or 1 large tomato - diced
½ onion - chopped
2 tbsp olive oil
1.5 tbsp brown sugar
½ tbsp Italian seasoning
1 8oz can of tomato sauce

3-4 slices of bacon - cooked and chopped

How to Make It

1. Chop all your veggies.
2. Heat EVOO in skillet over medium heat.
3. Add the rest of the ingredients to the skillet except the bacon.
4. Cook for 15-20 minutes or until veggies are cooked.
5. Cover with bacon and serve!

Veggie Mac n Cheese

What You Need

1 box GF mac n cheese
¼ cup milk
 2 tbsp butter
1 zucchini chopped
1 yellow squash chopped
¼ cup of chopped carrots
¼ cup milk
1 cup shredded cheddar cheese
salt & pepper

How to Make It

1. Heat oven to 350.
2. Cook the mac n cheese according to the instructions on the box, but shorten the cooking time to 8 minutes.
3. Continue to follow the box and add the butter and milk and cheese packet to the noodles.
4. Combine veggies, milk and half the cheese in a casserole dish.
5. Mix in the prepared mac n cheese and cover with remaining cheese.
6. Cook for 30-40 minutes.

This is a great way for kids to eat vegetables. Sometimes I even grate the vegetables so they are so small the kids can't see them!

Green Bean Casserole

What You Need

2 cans of green beans, drained
¼ cup chopped onions
1 tbsp butter
¾ cup sour cream
1 tsp salt
1 tsp sugar
1 cup shredded cheddar cheese

How to Make It

1. Heat oven to 350 degrees.
2. In a skillet over medium heat melt the butter and cook the onions for about 5 minutes.
3. Add salt, sugar, sour cream and beans.
4. Mix together and put in 8x8 casserole dish.
5. Cover with cheese and bake for 30 minutes.

Sweet Potato Casserole

What You Need

5 sweet potatoes
¼ cup butter
2 eggs
1 tsp GF vanilla
½ tsp cinnamon
¼ cup white sugar
2 tbsp milk
Salt

Topping
2 tbsp butter melted
2 tbsp GF flour
½ cup brown sugar
½ cup chopped pecans

How to Make It

1. Peel and cut up sweet potatoes into cubes and boil until soft, about 15 minutes.
2. Heat oven to 350 degrees.
3. Mash sweet potatoes and mix in butter, eggs, white sugar, milk, vanilla, cinnamon and salt. Put in a casserole dish.
4. To make topping: in a small bowl mix together melted butter, GF flour, brown sugar and pecans.
5. Spread topping over potatoes in casserole dish and bake for 30 minutes.

Ranch Potatoes

What You Need

4lbs of potatoes, cubed
1 small onion, chopped
4 tbsp butter, melted
Salt and pepper
Garlic salt

1 cup shredded cheddar cheese
3 tbsp ranch dressing
2 slices of bacon chopped up.

How to Make It

1. Heat oven to 400 degrees.
2. Grease a 9x13 casserole dish.
3. Put cubed potatoes and onions in dish and cover with seasonings to taste.
4. Pour melted butter over potatoes.
5. Cover with foil and cook for 45 minutes.
6. Take out of oven and mix in cheese and ranch. Then cover with bacon pieces.
7. Cook uncovered for 10 more minutes or until cheese melts.

Desserts

Cake Balls   70

Cheesecake   71

Christmas Crack   72

Monster Cookies   73

Pear Cobbler   74

Apple Pie   75

Pumpkin Whoopie Pies   76

Strawberry Cake   78

Cobbler   79

Lemon Squares   80

Cake Balls

What You Need

1 box of GF cake mix (white or chocolate)
     Ingredients on the box
1 jar of GF white icing
Melting chocolate
Sprinkles

How to Make It

1. Make cake as directed on box. Let cool at least 30 minutes.
2. Crumble cake. You can use your hands or a mixer.
3. Combine cake crumbs and icing. Use a spatula and your hands. Put in fridge for at least 30 minutes.
4. Form balls. You can use a dough scooper to get a consistent size or roll them out with your hands.
5. Freeze for at least 2 hours, overnight is fine.
6. Melt chocolate, coat balls in chocolate and decorate!

TIPS:
If the cake balls start to fall apart while you are coating them put them back in the freezer for a few minutes.

These could easily be turned into Cake Pops by inserting lollipop sticks into the balls at the end of Step 4.

Cheesecake

What You Need

Crust
1 bag of GF Ginger Snaps (8oz bag)
2 tbsp butter - melted

4 - 8oz GF cream cheese packages at room temperature
1 cup white sugar
3/4 cup milk
4 eggs
1 cup sour cream
1 tbsp GF vanilla extract
1/4 cup GF flour mix
Lemon zest of half a lemon

How to Make It

1. Heat oven to 350 degrees.
2. Grease the sides and bottom of the spring form pan.
3. Crush your ginger snaps. You can put them in a Ziploc bag and use a rolling pin to crush them. Mix crumbs with melted butter.
4. Press into spring form pan and let it go up the sides about 1/2 inch.
5. Mix together the sour cream, GF flour and GF vanilla extract in a bowl and set aside.
6. Mix together the cream cheese, sugar, milk, lemon zest and eggs. Mix in the sour cream mixture.
7. Fill pan and bake for 1 hour. Then turn off the oven **(don't open the door)** and leave it in the oven for at least 2 hours.
8. Once it is cooked let chill for at least 2 hours in the refrigerator before serving.

Christmas Crack

What You Need

1 ½ sticks of butter
1 ½ cups of brown sugar - unpacked
1 ½ tbsp Karo Syrup
1 ½ cups Cashews
7 cups of GF Rice & Corn Chex cereal mixed

How to Make It

1. Melt butter and brown sugar in large pot until bubbly stirring with a wooden spoon over medium heat. Once bubbles appear add in Karo Syrup and stir for 3 minutes.
2. Remove from heat and mix in cashews and cereal. Stir together gently so you don't break up the cereal.
3. Pour out onto wax or parchment paper to cool.
4. Once cooled you may need to break up any clumps. Put in tins, bags, etc and share!

This is what we make every Christmas for gifts for our co-workers and the kids teachers. We normally make at least six batches during the holidays. It is so good and very addictive!

Monster Cookies

What You Need

1/2 cup butter, softened
1/2 cup peanut butter
2 eggs
1 box Betty Crocker Gluten Free Cookie Mix
3/4 cup M&M's
1 cup Chex Rice Cereal
1 cup GF Rice Krispies

How to Make It

1. Heat oven to 350 degrees.
2. Mix butter, peanut butter and eggs.
3. Add cookie mix. (May need to add water if dough is too dry).
4. Stir in M&M's and cereal; be careful not to break up cereal.
5. Bake on parchment paper for 10-13 minutes.

Makes 18 cookies

Pear Cobbler

What You Need

2 cans of pears
1 cup GF flour
1 cup sugar
1 egg
1/2 box of raisins
1/2 cup milk
1 tsp cinnamon

How to Make It

1. Heat oven to 350 degrees.
2. Put drained pears into 8x8 dish and sprinkle with raisins.
3. In a bowl mix together the rest of the ingredients. You may need to add a little more milk if the batter isn't wet enough.
4. Pour batter over the pears.
5. Bake for 35-40 minutes or until top gets brown.

Serve warm with GF ice cream!

Apple Pie

What You Need

1 Gluten Free Pie crust
3 to 4 Large apples peeled, cored, and sliced
1/2 cup white sugar
1 tsp cinnamon
1/4 cup brown sugar

Topping
3/4 cup GF flour
1/3 cup white sugar
1/3 cup brown sugar
6 tbsp cold butter

How to Make It

1. Heat oven to 400 degrees.
2. Mix apples and other ingredients together.
3. Fill pie crust with apple and sugar mixture.
4. Mix sugar and flour together for topping. Cut in butter, use your fingers to mix it in.
5. Top the apple mixture with the topping.
6. Bake for 35 minutes.
7. Let cool 10 minutes then serve.

Pumpkin Whoopie Pies

What You Need

2 cups GF flour
1 tsp baking soda
½ tsp cinnamon
1½ tsp nutmeg
1½ tsp baking powder
½ tsp salt

1 cup packed brown sugar
1 stick butter - softened
¾ cup can pumpkin pie filling - unseasoned
¼ cup milk
1 egg
1 tsp GF vanilla

Filling:
4 oz cream cheese
1 tbsp butter - softened
½ tsp cinnamon
½ tsp GF vanilla
2 cups powdered sugar

How to Make It

1. Heat oven to 350 degrees.
2. Put dry ingredients (first 6 listed) in a bowl and set aside.
3. In a mixer combine brown sugar and butter. Cream together at medium speed.
4. Then add in pumpkin, milk, egg and GF Vanilla. Once this is combined slowly add in dry ingredients.

5. Place small balls of dough on parchment paper covered cookie sheet.
6. With a greased spoon press down on dough balls so the finished cookies will be flatter.
7. Cook for 11 minutes. Let cool completely.
8. To make filling- combine all ingredients but the powdered sugar together at medium speed in a blender.
9. Slowly add in powdered sugar.
10. Once cookies are cool spread filling onto one cookie and make a sandwich using a second cookie - bottom to bottom.

Makes 14 whoopie pies

Strawberry Cake

What You Need

1 box GF white cake mix
1 box GF strawberry Jell-O
½ cup cold water
4 eggs
1 cup vegetable oil
3 tbsp GF flour
2 cups chopped strawberries - fresh or thawed frozen

1 jar GF icing of choice

How to Make It

1. Heat oven to 325 degrees.
2. Grease and flour 9 x 11 pan.
3. Mix together Jell-O and water.
4. Using a mixer combine all ingredients for 2 minutes.
5. Pour into prepared pan and bake for 35 to 40 minutes or until toothpick comes out clean.
6. Cool completely and then decorate!

Cobbler

What You Need

1 16oz bag of frozen fruit
½ cup of butter melted
¾ cup of white sugar
1 cup GF flour
1 cup milk
2 tsp baking powder
¼ tsp salt

2 tbsp baking sugar crystals (Large sugar sprinkles)

How to Make It

1. Heat oven to 350 degrees.
2. Mix together all ingredients but fruit.
3. Pour fruit in casserole dish and cover with batter.
4. Cover with sugar crystals and bake for 50 minutes. If you prefer your cobbler to be gooey just cook for 40 minutes.
5. Serve with ice cream or whip cream.

This is my go to dessert for when guests come over. I always keep a bag of frozen fruit in the freezer so I can throw this together when needed.

Lemon Squares

What You Need

1 ½ cups GF flour
½ cup confectioners sugar
¾ cup butter
4 eggs
¾ cup sugar
juice of 2 lemons
zest of 1 lemon
1 tsp baking powder

How to Make It

1. Heat oven to 350 degrees.
2. Mix together GF flour and confectioners sugar.
3. Cut in the butter to flour and sugar mixture, use your hands.
4. Press dough into 9x13 or 2 9x9 pans. Use parchment paper or spray with GF cooking spray to avoid sticking.
5. Bake for 15 minutes.
6. Let sit for 10 minutes while you mix the lemon layer.
7. Mix together the remaining ingredients with a hand mixer
8. Pour over flour layer and cook for 20 minutes.
9. Cover with a dusting of confectioners sugar
10. Chill them for 2 hours before serving.

Index

Apple Pie   75

Bacon Cheeseburger Puffs   27
Bacon Ranch Puffs   23
Banana Pancakes   16
Baked Mozzarella Sticks   28
Baked Potato Skins   29
Baked Ziti   34
BBQ Chicken   57
BBQ Pork Chops   58
Beef Non-Stew   35
Beef Roast   61
Broccoli and Quinoa Bites   30

Cake Balls   70
Cheesecake   71
Chicken Fried Rice   37
Chicken Spaghetti   36
Chicken Tater Tot Casserole   49
Chicken with White Sauce   53
Christmas Crack   72
Cobbler   79
Corn Dog Muffins   31
Crock Pot Lasagna   54

Egg Frittatas   17
Enchilada Casserole   50

Hawaiian Pork   60

Greek Yogurt Pancakes 22
Green Bean Casserole 66

Lasagna 38
Lemon Squares 80

Meatloaf 39
Mexican Chicken Chili 59
Mexican Shepherd Pie 40
Monster Cookies 73

One Dish Wonder 41
Onion Rings 26
Overnight Oatmeal Smoothies 21

Parmesan Pork Chops 42
Pasta Bake 43
Pear Cobbler 74
Pepperoni Bake 44
Pumpkin Chocolate Chip Muffins 18
Pumpkin Whoopie Pies 76

Quinoa Pizza Treats 32

Ranch Potatoes 68

Sausage Balls 20
Sausage Breakfast Skillet 19
Sausage and Peppers 56
Scalloped Potato and Hamburger 45

Shepherd's Pie   46
Strawberry Cake   78
Stuffed Pepper Casserole   47
Stuffed Peppers   48
Summer Veggie Medley   64
Sweet Potato Casserole   67

Teriyaki Chicken   55

Veggie Mac n Cheese   65

Notes

Notes

Notes

Made in the USA
Charleston, SC
01 April 2013